P9-EER-645

BLAIRSVILLE SENIOR HIGH SCHOOL
BLAIRSVILLE, PENNA.

WOMEN WHO WIN

Laila Ali

Cynthia Cooper

Lindsay Davenport

Mia Hamm

Martina Hingis

Chamique Holdsclaw

Marion Jones

Anna Kournikova

Michelle Kwan

Lisa Leslie

Gabrielle Reece

Dorothy "Dot" Richardson

Sheryl Swoopes

Venus & Serena Williams

CHELSEA HOUSE PUBLISHERS

T 31939
L

WOMEN WHO WIN

Dorothy "Dot" Richardson

Heather Forkos

Introduction by
HANNAH STORM

CHELSEA HOUSE PUBLISHERS
Philadelphia

Frontis: Dot raises her fist in victory as the U.S. women's softball team breezes past Colombia 9-0 to earn a gold medal in the 1999 Pan American Games.

CHELSEA HOUSE PUBLISHERS

Editor in Chief: Sally Cheney
Director of Production: Kim Shinners
Production Manager: Pamela Loos
Art Director: Sara Davis
Production Editor: Diann Grasse

Staff for Dorothy "Dot" Richardson
Editor: Sally Cheney
Associate Editor: Benjamin Kim
Associate Art Director: Takeshi Takahashi
Layout by D&G Limited.

© 2001 by Chelsea House Publishers, a subsidiary of
Haights Cross Communications. All rights reserved.
Printed and bound in the United States of America.

The Chelsea House World Wide Web address is
http://www.chelseahouse.com

First Printing

1 3 5 7 9 8 6 4 2

Library of Congress Cataloging-in-Publication Data

Forkos, Heather.
 Dorothy "Dot" Richardson / Heather Forkos.
 p. cm.
 Includes bibliographical references (p.) and index.
 ISBN 0-7910-6535-9 (alk. paper)
 1. Richardson, Dot, 1961—Juvenile literature. 2. Women softball
 players—United States—Biography—Juvenile literature. I. Title.

GV865.R428 F67 2001
796.357'8—dc21
 [B]   2001028966

CONTENTS

WOMEN WHO WIN

Hannah Storm
NBC Studio Host

You go girl! Women's sports are the hottest thing going right now, with the 1900s ending in a big way. When the U.S. team won the 1999 Women's World Cup, it captured the imagination of all sports fans and served as a great inspiration for young girls everywhere to follow their dreams.

That was just the exclamation point on an explosive decade for women's sports—capped off by the Olympic gold medals for the U.S. women in hockey, softball, and basketball. All the excitement created by the U.S. national basketball team helped to launch the Women's National Basketball Association (WNBA), which began play in 1997. The fans embraced the concept, and for the first time, a successful and stable women's professional basketball league was formed.

I was the first ever play-by-play announcer for the WNBA—a big personal challenge. Broadcasting, just like sports, had some areas with limited opportunities for women. There have traditionally not been many play-by-play opportunities for women in sports television, so I had no experience. To tell you the truth, the challenge I faced was a little scary! Sometimes we are all afraid that we might not be up to a certain task. It is not easy to take risks, but unless we push ourselves we will stagnate and not grow.

Here's what happened to me. I had always wanted to do play-by-play earlier in my career, but I had never gotten the opportunity. Not that I was unhappy—I had been given studio hosting assignments that were unprecedented for a woman and my reputation was well established in the business. I was comfortable in my role . . . plus I had just had my first baby. The last thing I needed to do was suddenly tackle a new skill on national television and risk being criticized (not to mention, very stressed out!). Although I had always wanted to do play-by-play, I turned down the assignment twice, before reluctantly agreeing to give it a try. During my hosting stint of the NBA finals that year, I traveled back and forth to WNBA preseason games to practice play-by-play. I was on 11 flights in 14 days to seven different cities! My head was spinning and it was no surprise that I got sick. On the day of the first broadcast, I had to have shots just so I could go on the air without throwing up. I felt terrible and nervous, but I survived my first game. I wasn't very good but gradually, week by week,

I got better. By the end of the season, the TV reviews of my work were much better—*USA Today* called me "most improved."

During that 1997 season, I witnessed a lot of exciting basketball moments, from the first historic game to the first championship, won by the Houston Comets. The challenge of doing play-by-play was really exciting and I loved interviewing the women athletes and seeing the fans' enthusiasm. Over one million fans came to the games; my favorite sight was seeing young boys wearing the jerseys of female players—pretty cool. And to think I almost missed out on all of that. It reinforced the importance of taking chances and not being afraid of challenges or criticism. When we have an opportunity to follow our dreams, we need to go for it!

Thankfully, there are now more opportunities than ever for women in sports (and other areas, like broadcasting). We thank women, like those in this series, who have persevered despite lack of opportunities—women who have refused to see their limitations. Remember, women's sports has been around a long time. Way back in 396 B.C. Kyniska, a Spartan princess, won an Olympic chariot race. Of course, women weren't allowed to compete, so she was not allowed to collect her prize in person. At the 1996 Olympic games in Atlanta, Georgia, over 35,600 women competed, almost a third more than in the previous Summer Games. More than 20 new women's events have been added for the Sydney, Australia, Olympics in 2000. Women's collegiate sports continues to grow,spurred by the 1972 landmark legislation Title IX, which states that "no person in the United States shall, on the basis of sex, be excluded from participation in, be denied the benefits of, or be subjected to discrimination under any educational program or activity receiving federal financial assistance." This has set the stage for many more scholarships and opportunities for women, and now we have professional leagues as well. No longer do the most talented basketball players in the country have to go to Europe or Asia to earn a living.

The women in this series did not have as many opportunities as you have today. But they were persistent through all obstacles, both on the court and off. I can tell you that Cynthia Cooper is the strongest woman I know. What is it that makes Cynthia and the rest of the women included in this series so special? They are not afraid to share their struggles and their stories with us. Their willingness to show us their emotions, open their hearts, bare their souls, and let us into their lives is what, in my mind, separates them from their male counterparts. So accept this gift of their remarkable stories and be inspired. Because you, too, have what it takes to follow your dreams.

1

ONE FOR THE RECORD BOOKS

Dot Richardson stood at home plate in the bottom of the first inning, bat ready, and watched in dismay as the first pitch from Puerto Rican pitcher Lisa Martinez hit the ground and rolled. She had wanted to hit that first pitch up into the bleachers, to turn it into the first home run in Olympic softball history. And she hadn't even gotten a chance to swing at it.

Dot was the leadoff batter, making her the first member of the U.S. team to bat in the Olympics. As the leadoff, she felt that she had a responsibility to set the tone for the team's offense. "My job is hitting it hard," she commented to reporters at the 1996 Olympics in Atlanta, Georgia. "I see my role: 'If Dot hits it hard, everybody hits hard.'" Dot had a special goal for leading the team in the first game of the Olympics: she wanted to hit the very first home run. While she was training for the Olympics, Dot had often dreamed that she hit the first home run of the Olympics off the very first pitch—and then went on to hit the home run that won the gold medal for the United States.

The pitcher wound up for another throw, spinning her arm backwards in a complete circle before releasing the

Spirits run high as Dot and teammates Laura Berg (right) and Lisa Fernandez (left) celebrate Dot's two-run homer against China in the 1996 Olympic gold medal game.

ball. Crack! Dot singled, hitting the ball so hard that it bounced off two players' gloves. She sprinted to first base. The next batter, U.S. pitcher Julie Smith, bunted the ball, tapping it lightly into the infield. The bunt gave Dot time to get to second base, but Julie was called out at first. When a wild pitch got past the catcher's mitt, Dot ran to third while the Puerto Rican catcher was scrambling for the loose ball. U.S. pitcher Lisa Fernandez made the hit that sent Dot home to score the first run in Olympic softball history—off of a single to right field.

Lisa Fernandez, a long-time friend of Dot's, had ties to both of the teams that played in the first Olympic softball game. Her mother is Puerto Rican, and Lisa once played softball for Puerto Rico. However, she was determined to play her best regardless of her opponent.

"I know my heritage," she told the *Atlanta Journal-Constitution*. "My heart is in the USA. If someone asks me my nationality, I say I'm Cuban [on her father's side] and Puerto Rican. But as a softball player, I'm an American. When you step on the field, hey, your opponent is your opponent. Nothing matters except winning that game." Fernandez also scored, and after the first inning, the United States led 2-0.

Leading the U.S. team's defense that day was left-handed pitcher Michelle Granger, who pitched the entire game for the U.S. team. Granger, 20, had the honor of throwing the first pitch in Olympic softball history—a strike against Puerto Rican batter Lourdes Baez. Her fastballs zoomed across the plate at 70 mph. Because softball players stand closer to the pitcher's mound than major league baseball players, Michelle's opponents have just as little time to react to her fastballs as Randy Johnson's do to his.

Pitcher Lisa Fernandez jumps for joy after the final out to defeat the Chinese team for the gold medal at the 1996 Olympics. Lisa's 70 mph fastball pitches were an important part of the women's team victory.

Michelle threw merciless fastballs in the top of the second inning. Three batters stepped to the plate to face her, and all three struck out. The bottom of the second inning was also scoreless, but the U.S. scored three times in the bottom of the third. After Lisa Fernandez scored the third run of the game for the U.S., Puerto Rico took Lisa Martinez out of the game and replaced her with pitcher Lisa Mize. U.S. catcher Gillian Boxx stepped to the plate. With the bases loaded, she hit a single off Mize to center field, driving in teammates Sheila Cornell and Kim Maher. The U.S. now led 5-0.

Mize and Puerto Rico were up against very powerful opponents. The United States was the strong favorite to win the gold medal. The U.S. national team had a record of 110-1 in World Championship and Pan American Games competition for the ten years preceding the Olympics. Often, they beat their opponents by as much as 20–30 runs! The U.S. had won gold medals in many international competitions, including the International Softball Federation (ISF) Women's World Championship, the World Challenger Cup, and the Pan American Games (a tournament similar to the Olympics in which only teams from countries in North and South America compete). Many of the women on the 1996 U.S. Olympic team, including Dot, had played on these winning teams. The team won 59 of the 60 exhibition games they played while touring the United States in preparation for the Olympics.

Despite the stiff competition, Puerto Rico managed to hold the United States scoreless during the fourth and fifth innings. At the bottom of the sixth inning, Dot stepped to the plate for her fourth at-bat. BAM—a line drive over the center field fence—the first home run of softball Olympic history! "It doesn't get any better than this," thought Dot as she watched the ball soar 200 feet before disappearing behind the fence. And then she thought, "It's *gonna* get better than this." As she rounded the bases, her arms spread out in victory, she scanned the faces in the crowd. "I was looking for my parents in the stands as I came around, because they knew what I had dreamed and talked so much about," she later told reporters. When she reached home, she embraced on-deck hitter Julie Smith in a victory hug.

"In my dream I actually hit it (the home run) on the first pitch of the game, but I will take them any way they come," Dot joked. A volunteer security guard retrieved the home-run ball and handed it to Dot's parents as a souvenir.

Dot's home run touched off a U.S. hitting streak. Later that inning, Sheila Cornell hit a double to right field that sent Lisa Fernandez home. The U.S. scored three more times to bring the score to 10-0. At that point, the umpires declared the game a victory for the U.S. under a 10-run mercy rule, even though only six of the seven innings had been played. A mercy rule ends a game early if one team is beating the other by large number of runs. The Puerto Ricans had gotten only got two hits against Michelle Granger.

The U.S. players were pleased and proud of their performance. After the game, Lisa Fernandez told the *Colorado Springs Gazette-Telegraph*, "Today, I felt like I was representing the United States, but also representing Puerto Rico. That made it a tough game as well as an emotional game. But I'm proud to be a part of this team. We've given so much to reach this special moment."

The day was especially meaningful for Michelle Smith. Exactly ten years earlier, to the day, Michelle nearly lost her pitching arm when she was thrown from her father's pickup truck in a terrifying accident. "In 1986 I was faced with the reality that I might never pitch again. Sometimes it's hard for me to believe that after everything that happened, my Olympic dream actually came true," said Smith in the book

Etched in Gold: The Story of America's First-Ever Olympic Gold Medal Winning Softball Team.

Michelle wasn't the only player who thought she might never get to play in the Olympics. "When we [the softball team] didn't make it into the games in '92," Dot, at 34 years of age the oldest member of the 1996 Olympic team, told *Esquire* magazine, "I felt like I'd missed my last shot at the Olympics."

As a small child, Dot dreamed of playing softball in the Olympics—long before softball became an Olympic sport. "I've dreamed about being in the Olympics since I was 6," she told the *L.A. Times*. "People thought I chose the wrong sport because all the rest that I played [such as volleyball and basketball] were in the Olympics." In 1976, at the age of 15, Dot had the opportunity to join the first women's professional fast-pitch softball league, but she turned it down because, at that time, professional athletes were ineligible for the Olympics, and she hoped that one day softball would become an Olympic sport. As a 13-year-old, the youngest person ever to play in Amateur Softball Association (ASA) Women's Major Fast-Pitch League, Dot had the opportunity to play with some of the pioneers of her sport. Dot understood the debt of gratitude that the 1996 Olympic team owed to the women who had come before them—women who had played softball before their efforts could earn them college scholarships, endorsement money, or an Olympic medal.

"You cry for the people who didn't make it who are deserving and for those who played before you who weren't in any Olympic games," Dot said in an interview with *Southern Living* magazine, given after the Olympic team had

Victory on the field. There are hugs all around as the U.S. women beat China 1-0 and advance to the 1996 Olympic championship game.

been named. "I hope and pray that anyone who has ever seen me, played against me, or played with me knows I'm there to represent her."

Dot's winning attitude has done as much for her sport as her hitting and fielding have. She has conducted herself graciously as a representative of her country and her sport, continuously giving of herself to help younger players achieve their dreams, now that her own greatest dream, winning the gold medal, has been achieved. She has hung that medal around the necks of many children, to inspire them to reach for the gold themselves. She works with young athletes in softball clinics and with coaches through the Dot Richardson Softball Association, an instructional league that emphasizes teaching the basic skills of the game. She also has her own line of instructional videotapes.

In *Etched in Gold*, Dot said simply, "There would be no Dot Richardson, Olympian, if the great players in the past had not taken the time to help a 10-year-old kid learn the game."

2

AN ORLANDO REBEL

Dorothy Gay Richardson was born on September 22, 1961, in Orlando, Florida to Ken and Joyce Richardson. Even as a baby, her family couldn't believe how much energy and spirit she had. On a family trip from Orlando to California, her parents joked in *Sports Illustrated*, Dot crawled around the family car so much that her parents finally put her in a box to keep her in one place (before laws were passed requiring all babies to ride in car seats). "Dorothy never walked as a baby," her mother Joyce remembered. "She ran."

Dorothy (who is often called "Dot," which is short for "Dorothy") was born into a family of athletes. "My dad was a football, baseball, track-and-field, and basketball player," Dot told *Southern Living*. "My mom was a cheerleader who ran faster than my dad, so he says." Dorothy has two older sisters, Kathy and Laurie; an older brother, Kenny; and a younger brother, Lonnie, all of whom are also athletic. As a child, Dot played sports with her brothers whenever possible. Her natural talent at catching, throwing, and

After demoralizing losses to Japan, China, and Australia in the 1996 Olympics, Dot's team was nearly forced out of medal contention. But in consecutive wins against Cuba, Italy, Australia, and Japan, Dot showed her talents and helped lead her team to gold.

kicking was evident in every sport she tried. "I feel that God has given me this talent with my hands," Dot said in *People* magazine. She also has unusually sharp vision and can evaluate the rotation of a fastball as it speeds through the air toward the plate.

As a child, Dot loved football and wished she could be on a team like her older brother Kenny. When the family lived in England, Kenny's friends let 7-year-old Dot play goalie for their soccer team. Although the neighborhood kids let her play, organized sports were closed to Dot—because she was a girl. Girls often couldn't play in organized leagues when Dot was growing up in the 1960s. Until 1974, when Dot was 12, Little League teams wouldn't accept girls. "I'd understand if I didn't have a strong arm," Dot told the *New York Times Magazine*, "but I was just as good as the boys, if not better." Instead, Dot went to all of her brothers' Little League games and played around on the sidelines with an extra baseball. Her dad made her bat girl for her brothers' baseball team so that she would be allowed to practice with the boys and learn the skills that they were learning.

Dot's father Ken was an Air Force mechanic, and his job required the family to move around a lot when Dot was little. Dot has lived in Kansas, England, New Mexico, and Guam, among other places. When Dot was 10, her father retired and moved the family home to Orlando. It was in Orlando, while hanging around the Little League fields where her brothers were playing, that Dot was invited to join her first organized baseball team.

Dot was pitching to her brothers before the game when a coach who had been watching

told her he would love to have her on his team. All she had to do, he said, was cut her hair short, call herself Bob, and pretend to be a boy. Rather than pretend to be something she wasn't, Dot turned him down.

Dot began to throw the ball around with another girl her age who had been left out, her friend Sunday Brown. Once again, a man who had been watching came up to the girls and asked Dot if she'd be interested in joining a team. He introduced Dot to the coach of the Union Park Jets, an Amateur Softball Association (ASA) Women's fast-pitch Class A team. The coach asked Dot if she had ever played softball before. Dot didn't even know what softball was!

But softball is very similar to baseball, and that was a sport Dot knew very well. Most of the major rules are the same. The same positions are played, and the players stand in the

An inspiration to young women athletes everywhere, Dot takes time out to sign a few autographs for her fans at the Coca-Cola USA Softball Women's National Team Festival in 1998.

same places on the field. The object of the games is the same: To score runs by hitting the ball, and then to run around the bases without being called "out." If the ball is caught before it touches the ground, the batter is out. The games have the same number of players on the field (nine). These players try to catch the ball when hit. If they can't catch it, they try to tag the runner out (usually at one of the bases). In both games, each team is given three outs per inning.

One team bats until three of its players have been called out. Then the teams switch positions, and the team that was on the field gets a chance to bat. The first half of an inning is called the "top" of the inning and the second half is called the "bottom." Once each team has had a turn at bat, the inning is over. A standard baseball game has nine innings; a standard softball game has seven.

The main differences are the size of the ball, the pitching style, and the size of the field. A softball is approximately 12 inches in circumference, whereas a baseball is approximately 9 inches in circumference. In softball, the pitcher uses a windmill pitching style, rotating the arm backwards and releasing the ball underhand. Baseball pitchers release the ball overhand. The distance between the bases is shorter (90 feet in baseball versus 60 feet in softball), and so is the distance between the pitcher's mound and home plate (approximately 60 feet in baseball versus 40 feet in softball). One of the other main differences is that softball is played primarily by women. Baseball, especially at the college and professional levels, is still played primarily by men.

The coach sent Dot over to third base, where she fielded a few balls and got the feel of the softball. She didn't realize that she had just been given a tryout. The coach was shocked when she learned that Dot was only 10; most of the women on the team were in their 20s! But, realizing what a rare and valuable learning opportunity playing on the team would be for Dot, her parents agreed to let her do it.

Dot soon learned to ignore the age gap and began to focus on developing her skills. "I never think of age. It does not really matter how old you are—it matters how well you play," she recalled telling reporters in *Living the Dream*. But everybody was impressed with a thirteen-year-old who was one of the best players on an adult team. Fans even asked for her autograph! She became the leadoff hitter and starting third baseman for the team and was named to the league's All-Star team at the end of the season.

But one day, while fooling around in her yard, Dot cut her foot on a rusty sickle. The injury kept her from playing on the All-Star team. Instead, her mother signed her up for the Orlando Rebels instructional league after her foot had healed. The Orlando Rebels were an ASA Women's Major League softball team. Dot received instruction from Major League softball players and coaches, including Rebels head coach Marge Ricker. She said later in *Living the Dream* that this instruction may have been an even more important opportunity than being an All-Star. Ricker invited Dot to be a bat girl for the Rebels. Dot challenged herself to pick up the bats as fast as she could and studied the players' skills as she watched the games.

In 1975, Marge Ricker promoted Dot from bat girl to official member of the Orlando Rebels! Dot, age 13, would be the youngest player in history to play in softball's Major Leagues.

The Rebels traveled around the South in a motor home, mainly playing against teams in the Atlanta Coast League. Dot had a blast on the road. She sang along to the radio as the miles went by and spent her meal money on chocolate shakes and donuts. She would get so wound up in anticipation of the games that she couldn't sleep the night before a game. In one unforgettable game against the Stratford (Connecticut) Raybestos Brakettes—a team renowned for its many world-class players—Dot got a hit off of legendary pitcher Joan Joyce. Nobody on either team could believe that 13-year-old Dot, who had Joyce's auto-graph at home, had actually gotten a hit off of her hero! She played against other legends of the sport, too—players like Snookie Molder (her teammate on the Rebels), Irene Shea, and Sharron Backus (who later would be Dot's coach in college).

In 1972, President Richard Nixon signed an important law called Title IX, which made dis-crimination on the basis of sex in hiring, public school admissions, and other areas illegal. Title IX required that schools give boys and girls equal opportunities to play sports. Schools had to have the same number of boys' sports teams and girls' sports teams, and had to give those teams equal amounts of money. If a girl wanted to play a sport and there was no girls' team available, boys' teams would be required by law to accept girls. (Dot, for example, was allowed to participate on the boys' track team in the seventh grade.) Girls' sports teams and pro-grams were founded in record numbers all across the country (and all over the world, as similar laws were soon passed in other coun-tries, such as Australia and Canada).

When she was in the seventh grade, Dot tried out for the cheerleading squad after her classmates had teased her for being a tomboy; Dot wanted them to know that she could be feminine too. Dot wasn't picked to cheer for the boys' teams, but not making the squad gave her the chance to play for four of the girls' teams—volleyball, basketball, softball (slow-pitch), and track. She performed so well that she was awarded the school's Most Valuable Player award in each sport. It was no surprise that she was the first girl to win the school's Outstanding Athlete of the Year Award. Eventually, Dot learned not to pay attention to what people said about her.

Dot continued to dominate multiple sports teams at Colonial High School in Orlando, where she played volleyball, track, softball, basketball, and tennis. Her high school had a slow-pitch softball team—in which the pitches are slower because the windmill style of pitching is not used—but Dot still enjoyed the games. She batted left-handed for fast-pitch games and right-handed for slow-pitch games.

In the summers, she continued to play for the Rebels. In 1976, tennis legend Billie Jean King and Joan Joyce formed the International Women's Professional Softball Association, the first women's professional softball league. Dot was on the protected list for a team called the Connecticut Falcons. Although Dot declined the opportunity to play for the league, hoping to be in the Olympics one day, several of her teammates joined the newly–formed Orlando Suns. Dot became a starter and the leadoff batter for the Rebels.

Dot was also an outstanding student and a member of National Honor Society. In her

As a warm-up for the 2000 Olympics in Australia, Dot and the U.S. women's team played an exhibition game against a team of collegiate all-stars. Dot's willingness to meet any challenge has proven an invaluable asset in her quest for Olympic gold.

senior year in high school, as in junior high, she won Most Valuable Player awards in every sport she played and Outstanding Athlete of the Year. Again, it was the first time that a girl had won this honor (which the coaches, reluctant to give the honor to a girl, decided to award to both a male and a female athlete).

"There's a drive within my family to see how high you can go and what you can reach," Dot told *Southern Living*. "My advice to youngsters is always, 'Feel like you've given your best, on the field and off.'"

3

"A LESSON OF BALANCE"

While in high school, Dot fantasized about attending the University of California at Los Angeles (UCLA), which had won national titles in volleyball, basketball, softball, and track—all of which were Dot's sports. But UCLA was over 3,000 miles away, and Dot's parents wanted her closer to home. Many schools recruited her for both fast-pitch and slow-pitch softball teams, but she preferred fast-pitch. She decided to attend Western Illinois University, which offered her a full scholarship to play softball. Western Illinois was closer to home than UCLA, and it had an excellent program in athletic training, which Dot planned to study.

In 1979, the summer after Dot graduated from high school, softball was played at the Pan American Games for the first time. Dot was honored to be invited to try out, but Coach Ricker warned her that she had little chance of making the team. Several weeks later, Dot found herself on a plane to San Juan, Puerto Rico, with the other members of the U.S. team. At age 17, she was the youngest starter on the team, which went on to win the gold medal.

You're outta here! Dot hangs on to make the tag out at second base against China's Qiu Haitao in the 2000 Olympics.

That fall, Dot began her freshman year at Western Illinois. She played field hockey (a sport she had never tried before), basketball, and softball, starting at shortstop. She led the country with a batting average of .480 and was nominated for a Broderick Award in softball (given to the best collegiate athlete in a given sport). She also volunteered to work with the school's physical therapist and thought about becoming a doctor.

When Dot learned that the coach at UCLA was interested in her, she decided to transfer to the school of her dreams. It was an excellent match. Dot thrived at UCLA. Playing and pre-med studies kept her very busy. "I would frequently be playing a doubleheader," she recalled in *People Weekly*, "and then sprinting to the opposite end of the campus for my chem lab. I'd still be in my uniform, dirty from sliding."

Dot led the team in hitting, was given the team's Most Valuable Player award, and was named an NCAA All American all three years that she played for UCLA. "Other coaches often told their pitchers to walk her," said UCLA coach Sue Enquist in the book *Winning Women in Baseball & Softball*. "That way she couldn't do much damage, like hit a home run. Even if she was walked, her love of the game boosted the level of play for her teammates."

In the summer, Dot traveled home to play for the Orlando Rebels. In 1981, the Rebels rocked the softball world when they defeated the Raybestos Brakettes—who had dominated U.S. softball throughout the 1970s—in the national championships! Dot was awarded the Erv Lind award for being the best defensive player in the national championships—on either team.

UCLA played in the national collegiate championships in Dot's sophomore, junior, and senior years. In 1982, Dot's hitting and fielding skills, along with Debbie Doom's strong pitching, were key factors in UCLA's victory in the NCAA Championship. The following year, their hopes of defending their title were dashed when several members of the team got food poisoning during the national championships. Despite their illness, they didn't give up without a fight.

"Dottie was probably the sickest," Coach Enquist said. "I remember her hitting a ball into the outfield, stretching a single into a double, and vomiting on second base. She would not come out of the game. When you see someone with that kind of courage, it raises the entire team's game."

After graduation, Dot moved to New York and enrolled in a master's program in health at Adelphi University. There, Dot tried coaching for

Head Coach Ralph Raymond was the first to give Dot the nickname "Tiger" and coached her from her early days with the Raybestos Brakettes all the way to Olympic gold. As Dot struggled to overcome injuries and to balance her medical and athletic careers, Coach Raymond never stopped believing in her talent and determination.

the first time. She also began to play with the Raybestos Brakettes. The Brakettes had a long history of fielding the best athletes in the sport. They have won 24 national championships— more than any other softball team. Their coach at that time, Ralph Raymond, coached them to 17 of those championships. He has also had an outstanding career coaching the U.S. national team in international tournaments, including the 1996 and 2000 Olympic Games. He is the coach who gave Dot the nickname "Tiger."

Playing for the Brakettes became more difficult for Dot after she began medical school at the University of Louisville in Louisville, Kentucky, in 1989. She had always managed to balance her studies with softball, but she wasn't sure that it would be possible to continue her softball career while she was in medical school. She often thought that she would have to give up softball, but her team was very supportive of her hectic schedule. They understood that she would not always be able to make it to practices, or even to games.

"I'd fly cross-country, be picked up at the airport by a fan and driven to the field, changing clothes in the car because I didn't want to wear my uniform on the plane," Dot told *Southern Living*. "My teammates would see me running onto the field in the 2nd inning of a doubleheader game to jump in at shortstop."

Even though she had to squeeze softball in around her study schedule, Dot was still one of the best players in the game. She has been named an ASA All-American 16 times, and has won the Erv Lind Award seven times.

Dot uses what she has learned from softball in the operating room. "Sports has prepared me for my career in medicine, without a doubt,"

Dot once told the *Philadelphia Inquirer.* "Imagine getting a call that a helicopter is coming in with a trauma patient. You prepare for what's going to be in front of you just like you prepare for an opponent in a game.

"Where is the ball likely to be hit? How should you react? It's the same thing in medicine. What are you going to look for? Just like in a game, you have to devote your full concentration. That's what I've been prepared to do."

But Dot finally "dropped the ball" in 1990, when she was so focused on playing in the World Championships that she failed an important medical school exam. Although she had the option of re-taking the test, Dot decided to repeat that year of medical school.

"I felt I had focused too much on athletics," she said in *Winning Women in Baseball & Softball.* "After that letdown, I devoted myself to my classes. The next year I passed. It was a lesson of balance."

Dot passed up invitations to parties or the movies in order to study. She stopped practicing softball and devoted the extra time to medicine. Her dedication to her studies earned her academic honors and the chance to have a top-notch medical career. But she spent so much time with her books that when spring rolled around, she wasn't ready for softball. When she tried out for the 1991 Pan American team, it was obvious to the coaches that she was out of shape. She hoped that they would choose her for the team anyhow, but they didn't. Dot rooted for the U.S. team from the stands during the Pan American Games, but her pride was hurt.

Dot had always dreamed of being in the Olympics one day, even though it looked like

Team spirit. These two young fans show their support for Dot and the team with matching stars-and-stripes hats during the U.S.-Netherlands game at Golden Park in Columbus, Georgia (1996).

the demands of her medical career might crowd softball out of her life. In 1993, softball was finally added to the roster of Olympic Sports for the XXVI Olympiad in Atlanta, Georgia. The news reached Dot just as she was applying for an orthopedic residency program (a training program to become an orthopedic surgeon). Dot knew that it might not be possible to pursue both her dream of being an Olympian and her dream of being a surgeon—but how could she give either of them up?

"[During the interview process for an orthopedic residency] I told them I am willing to not go to the Olympics if it means losing my position, but I'm hoping that you realize how important it is to achieve my dream for an Olympic gold medal. And if you would like an

Olympian for your residency program, I'd be more than willing to be that person," she recalled in the *Los Angeles Times*. Luckily, the residency program to which Dot was matched was willing to support her Olympic dream. She had to work many extra hours to get enough time off for softball games and tournaments.

Dot trained for the Olympics in between long shifts at the hospital, where she was doing her residency at the University of Southern California. (Her shifts were sometimes 20 hours long)! Since she had to squeeze practice in when she had the time and couldn't always get to a gym, she used a large net and a batting tee to turn her bedroom into a makeshift batting cage. She also ran on a treadmill and lifted weights. To limit the noise she made during her batting practices, Dot wrapped tape around her bat.

"I'm amazed she can do it," said John Kumar, another orthopedic resident at the USC Medical Center. "I mean, the difficulty of putting in 80-100 hours a week . . . then go home and try to read and learn about surgeries she's trying to do, as well as put in the time she needs to be an athlete . . . "I have a hard time dealing with what I need to do and I am nowhere near as involved in athletics."

4

OLYMPIC GOLD

Over 600 softball players tried out for the U.S. Olympic team. On the first day of tryouts, Dot hyperextended her neck while batting. The injury continued to plague her throughout the tryouts, but she played the best she could. On her last at-bat of the Olympic tryouts, Dot hit a home run! The next morning, Dot was one of the 15 players and 5 alternates named to the Olympic softball team. Dot, who was 33 at the time, was the oldest player on the roster. Ralph Raymond was selected to be the head coach.

The week after tryouts ended, Dot ruptured a disk in her back. She was very worried that she would have to give up her place on the team, her career as a surgeon, or both. She was afraid to tell the Olympic officials, who might replace her with an alternate, or even her colleagues at the hospital in California, who might tell her to drop softball before another injury ended her medical career.

For a few months, Dot's right arm was so weak that she couldn't hold a bat straight out in front of her. But after four months of working with a trainer, the arm slowly healed.

Wearing broad smiles and their hard-earned gold medals, Dot and teammates Lisa Fernandez and Shelly Stokes celebrate their victory during the 1996 Olympic medal ceremony.

Both an orthopedic surgeon and a winning Olympian, Dot has applied the same grit and determination to all her endeavors.

The Olympic team toured the country for a few months, playing exhibition games, before the Olympics began in Atlanta. The tour helped the team learn to work together and brought a taste of the Olympics to people around the country. The team signed autographs, made promotional appearances, and conducted free softball clinics. They won 59 of the 60 exhibition games they played (losing one game early in the tour to a team in Los Angeles).

After the tour, the athletes returned to their Olympic home—Fort Benning, Georgia. The Olympic softball games weren't played in Atlanta at all! Because no suitable park could be found in Atlanta, softball was played at Golden Park in Columbus, Georgia, a town 100 miles away from Atlanta. Instead of living at the Olympic Village, where most of the other Olympic athletes lived during the Games, the softball players were quartered at Fort Benning. This unusual arrangement, as Dot recalled in *Living the Dream*, had its positive side—the team was sheltered from the distractions of the Olympic Village and could focus on the game.

The U.S. team beat Puerto Rico 10-0 in the historic first softball game of Olympic history. The first round would be round-robin (each team would play against every other team). The top four teams would compete in the semifinals—the team with the best record (the #1 team) would play the #2 team; the #3 team would play the #4 team. The winner of the #3-#4 game would play the loser of the #1-#2 game in the finals (in the bronze medal game). The winner of that game would go on to play the #1 team in the gold medal game; the other team would receive the bronze medal.

In their second game, the United States faced the Netherlands. Starting pitcher Christa Williams, who had recently graduated from high school and who was, at age 18, the youngest player on the team, threw a two-hitter, and both Dot and first baseman Sheila

Cornell hit three-run homers for the U.S., leading the U.S. to a 9-0 victory over the Netherlands.

Their next game was against Japan, which had unexpectedly beaten China the day before. Japan wasn't so lucky against the Americans, although they were the first team that managed to score against the American pitchers. Michele Smith, the starting pitcher for the U.S., had played several seasons in the Japan League as an employee of Toyota and was fluent in Japanese. She knew her opponents well and was able to understand the Japanese coaches' instructions to their players. Haruko Saito hit a home run against Michele Smith in the fifth inning, but the Americans countered with two home runs of their own, hit by left fielder Kim Maher and center fielder Laura Berg. Smith pitched an excellent game, allowing only three hits, and the U.S. won the game 6-1.

Outstanding pitching was the key to the American's success. The U.S. had five pitchers whose fastballs reached 70 mph (or close to it): Lisa Fernandez, Michele Granger, Lori Harrigan, Michele Smith, and Christa Williams. "A lot of people thought the Americans would waltz to the gold in Atlanta." Michele Smith later told *Women's Sports and Fitness.* "We players knew better . . . one bad pitch can lose a game, one clutch hit can win one."

That's exactly what happened in dramatic match between the United States and Australia. Pitching for Australia was Tanya Harding, a very talented pitcher who had led UCLA to the NCAA National Championships in 1995. The United States had saved its best pitcher, Lisa Fernandez, for the challenging

Dot's long-time friend and teammate Lisa Fernandez winds up her power pitch in the Olympic final against Japan in the 2000 Olympics at Sydney, Australia.

match. Unfortunately, the U.S. team had gotten almost no sleep the night before, due to a game against Canada that had lasted until 2:30 A.M.

Lisa and Tanya kept the game scoreless for the first four innings. In the fifth inning, Dani Tyler smashed a home run over the center-field fence to give the U.S. team a 1-0 lead. But Dani had barely reached the dugout when the Australians were demanding that the umpire call her out, saying that she had forgotten to step on the plate. Video replays confirmed that Dani had failed to step on the plate, and she was called out. Dot stormed onto the field to protest the call. In *Living the Dream*, she explained that, although she had never yelled at an umpire before, she wanted Dani to know that her team was behind her and willing to fight for her.

The score remained 0-0, and the U.S., although demoralized by the loss of the home run, was by no means out of the game. After seven innings, the score was still tied, and Lisa Fernandez had yet to allow an Australian to get on base. If Dani's home run hadn't been thrown out, the U.S. would have won the game 1-0 after seven innings. Instead, the game went into overtime.

According to an international tie-breaker rule, when a game goes into extra innings in softball, the team at bat gets to start a player at second after the 9th inning. The rule is meant to encourage scoring and end the game more quickly. Lisa Fernandez kept her perfect game going until the tenth inning. The last person up to bat for Australia was Joanne Brown. With two outs, and two strikes against her, Joanne hit a home run and won the game for Australia!

The U.S. team's 5-0 winning streak already had guaranteed them a position in the semifinal round even before the loss. However, the loss meant that the U.S. had to beat the Chinese the following day to enter the semifinals as the #1 team. The Chinese, who many considered the U.S.'s biggest competition for the gold medal, put up a good fight. In the bottom of the second, catcher Gillian Boxx hit a sacrifice fly with the bases loaded to score Kim Maher for a 1-0 lead. Unfortunately, when Dot struck out to end the inning, three runners were left stranded on base. (At the highest level of play, it's often difficult to get a runner on base at all; a stranded runner is looked upon as a squandered opportunity to score.) They ended the following inning the same way—with three runners stranded and a score of 1-0. When China's Xuquing Liu hit a home run in the sixth inning, she gave China a 2-1 lead. Fortunately, Sheila Cornell hit a two-run homer in the bottom of the sixth inning to give the U.S. the win, 3-2.

The four teams that made it to the semifinals were Australia (5 wins, 2 losses), China (5 wins, 2 losses), Japan (5 wins, 2 losses), and the United States (6 wins, 1 loss). In the first semifinal match, the U.S. beat China 1-0. "We had some misfortunes," Lisa Fernandez told the *L.A. Times*. "But we fought back." The game went to ten innings, during which the U.S. stranded 10 runners. A bases-loaded single by Sheila Cornell in the bottom of the tenth sent Dot home for the game-winning run. China

Racing toward Olympic gold, U.S. team members Laura Berg, Dot Richardson, and Leah O'Brien-Amico leave the field grinning after their 2-0 defeat of New Zealand during the 2000 games. Never considering herself a solo superstar, Dot always gives her teammates full credit for their roles in each victory.

went on to the bronze medal game, and the U.S. to the gold medal game.

Australia defeated Japan in the other semifinal game, but lost to China in the bronze medal game. China advanced to the gold medal round to face the United States for the third time.

Golden Park was filled to capacity for the historic gold-medal face-off. Among the 8,750 fans filling the stands were a number of legendary softball players who had pioneered the sport—Joan Joyce, Diane Schumacher, Snookie Mulder, Kathy Arendsen, Marge Ricker, Stephanie Tenney, Irene Shea, and many others. As a young girl, Dot had played with some of them, and while the team was warming up, these legends passed down to the dugout a softball that they had autographed as a gift for her. It was the beginning of a magical game.

Michele Granger was the starting pitcher for the U.S. The first two innings were uneventful. In the top of the third, Chunfang Zhang got on base with a single. Zhang advanced to second when teammate Fang Yan singled. She stole third and then attempted to steal home, but was called out on a split-second throw from Dot. (In fact, the play was so close that even TV replays couldn't determine decisively whether or not Zhang had managed to touch the plate ahead of the tag).

Laura Berg singled in the bottom of the third, and Dot stepped up to the plate. Twice before, Dot had struck out against China. She let the first two pitches go by. The third pitch hurled toward her was a change-up (a slow pitch meant to throw the hitter's timing off). But it didn't fool Dot . . . Crack went the bat against the ball. As she headed to first, Dot was careful not to block the umpire's view. The ball sailed across the field into the stands behind right field, just inside the foul post. Home run! It was the gold-medal-winning home run of her dreams! The crowd shouted, "U.S.A., U.S.A." as Dot rounded the bases. Her teammates swarmed around her at the plate.

The Chinese protested the call for 10 full minutes. "I knew it was fair," Dot said in the *L.A. Times*. "I felt bad that they felt bad." The home run was ruled fair over the protests of the Chinese team. There were four innings left to play. The Chinese gave up one more run in the third inning, giving the U.S. a 3-0 lead. In the sixth inning, Coach Raymond removed Michele Granger from the mound and sent in Lisa Fernandez. The Chinese were positioned to score, with two outs and runners on second and third, and Raymond wanted his best pitcher in the game. The first pitch Lisa threw bounced off catcher Gillian Boxx's glove, allowing the runner on third to score. But Lisa wasn't about to let the gold medal slip away. She struck the next batter out for the third out to retire the side. But China held the U.S. scoreless in the bottom of the sixth, and the gold medal was still up for grabs.

The first batter for the Chinese hit a grounder but didn't make it safely to first. The second struck out. China's Jian Xu stepped to the plate. Strike one . . . strike two . . . strike three! The U.S. had won the gold! Dot's teammates piled one on top of the other in a celebratory group hug before lining up to shake hands with the Chinese players. During the medal ceremony, Dot cried when she saw the American flag being hoisted above the others and heard "The Star-Spangled Banner" begin to play.

Incredible as it might sound, Dot had to fly back to L.A. the following day to resume her residency at the hospital. For the first time in her life, Dot was recognized by complete strangers—everywhere! But it wasn't straight back to work for Dr. Dot. She was given a huge welcome back at the hospital—and another week off. Dot got to be a guest on *Late Night with David Letterman*, participate in the Walt Disney World Parade, and visit the First Family at the White House. Dot gave every child in the Children's Hospital a chance to try on her gold medal, to inspire their own dreams.

Her greatest dream had really come true.

5

"A Shining Light"

Twenty-four years passed between the day that Dot first played for the Union Park Jets and the day that she first played for the U.S. Olympic softball team. In between, Dot had represented the U.S. four times each in the Pan American Games and the World Championships (and had one silver and seven gold medals to show for it). She'd been named an ASA All-American 11 times and won the ASA's Erv Lind Award (for being the best defensive player in the Women's Majors national championship) seven times. She was the first female softball player to have her own signature bat. And, after leading UCLA to a national championship and being named a collegiate All-American three times, she'd been named NCAA Player of the Decade for the 1980s.

So she was a bit surprised to be dropped from the national team for two years after the Olympic victory. "That was very difficult, feeling unwanted," Dot later told the *Fort Worth Star-Telegram.* "I was hurt. But I think everything happens for a reason." It's possible that the

Dot's winning attitude is as important to women's sports as are her talents on the field. As a gracious representative of her country and her sport, she is always eager to donate her time to help younger players achieve their dreams.

national team coaches wanted to see how the team would do without Dot's leadership and were worried that they had become too dependent on it.

Dot finished her residency and became a full-fledged surgeon. Her hospital schedule kept her very busy—and so did her public speaking events, softball clinics, endorsements, and, as always, playing softball. She led the California Commotion to the 1997, 1998, and 1999 ASA National Championships. She later returned to the U.S. national team and won a gold medal at the 1999 Pan American Games.

The Olympics opened up many new endorsement opportunities for Dot. She signed contracts with Coca-Cola, Bausch & Lomb, Louisville Slugger, Rawlings® Sporting Goods, and Reebok, among others. Dot helped Rawlings design a softball glove that was marketed under her name. Despite softball's growing popularity, these companies paid Dot a fraction of what the top male professional athletes can earn in endorsements.

In 1997, Dot founded the Dot Richardson Softball Association (DRSA). The organization teaches coaches about how to manage a team and teach their players the fundamental skills of the game. Softball leagues affiliated with DRSA emphasize education in the basic skills of the sport and help players become well-rounded individuals.

The Women's Professional Softball League (WPSL) was also founded in 1997. The field was slightly larger than a standard ASA softball field. The pitcher's mound was six feet farther from home plate, and as WPSL pitcher Debbie Doom told the *Arizona Republic*, "It's a very big change . . . They wanted more offense in the league and they got it." Because the ball had to travel a greater distance from the mound to the plate, the ball was traveling slightly slower by the time it reached the plate and so was easier to hit. This increased scoring and made the games more exciting to watch.

In 1999, the rule banning professional softball players from competing in the Olympics was changed, making WPSL players eligible for the 2000 Olympic Games. Among the players this affected was 22-year-old Crystl Bustos. Bustos, who played shortstop, was an incredibly powerful hitter who frequently hit home runs. She led the Orlando Wahoos to the 1998 WPSL championship and was named the league's Most Valuable Player. She tied for most home runs (10) in the 1998 season and was among the league's leaders in several other offensive categories.

Dot and Crystl competed against each other for spots on the 2000 Olympic team. "It's really neat to see Dot out there," Crystl told reporters at the *Colorado Springs Gazette*. "She's been playing for 20-something years. It's something to shoot for." Both made the team, but Crystl would start at shortstop—Dot would start at second base. Dot had a year between tryouts and the Olympics to learn her new position.

Julie Smith, who had played second base for the 1996 Olympic team, did not make the 2000 team. She protested the results, but she remained on the sidelines. The controversy got the 2000 team off to a bit of a rocky start.

Doctor Dot is #1! Richardson swings and connects in Team USA's 10-0 defeat of the St. Louis All-Stars in August 2000.

In 2000, the Summer Olympics were held in Sydney, Australia. Because Australia is in the Southern hemisphere, its seasons are the opposite of those in the United States. When it's summer in the United States, it's winter in Australia. For this reason, the 2000 Summer Games didn't begin until September.

Softball received little television coverage during the 1996 Olympic Games. "They didn't televise the gold medal game in 1996, but what a small price to pay to get every game on TV in 2000," Dot told the *Detroit Free Press*. Because of the time difference between the United States and Australia (15 hours' difference between New York and Sydney), the games had to be broadcast the day after they were actually played.

The United States won its first game against Canada, 6-0. Once again, Dot hit a home run in the first game (along with teammates Crystl Bustos and Jennifer Brundage). Lori Harrigan pitched a no-hitter—the first in Olympic history. Their second game, against Cuba, also went smoothly. After only two games, Bustos had 3 home runs!

Christa Williams was the starting pitcher in the third game, against Japan. The U.S. team wasted many opportunities to score. They loaded the bases in the first, seventh, eighth, and ninth innings, but failed to drive any of those runners home.

"All the hype and attention are new and exciting," Dot told the L.A. Times, "but it's also adding new pressure we haven't faced."

Disaster struck in the eleventh inning. Haruko Saito, lead-off batter for Japan, hit a ground ball to Dot, whose throw to first base was off-target. Hiroko Tamoto—who had started the inning on second base due to the international tie-breaker rule—scored and brought the score to 1-0. The next batter, Misako Ando, hit the ball to left field. When the ball bounced off fielder Leah O'Brien's shoe, Saito advanced to third base, and Ando took off for second. Catcher Stacey Nuveman shot the ball across the diamond to Dot at second, but the ball bounced off her glove, giving Saito the opportunity to score. The U.S. scored a run in the bottom of the inning, but ended up losing the game 2-1. The team—and the world, which was watching this time—was stunned.

Lisa Fernandez, one of the team's strongest hitters and arguably the best player in the world, was upset with herself for striking out repeatedly with runners on base. Most of the team, in fact, had been hitting poorly. However, she was determined to shrug off the loss. "This is just a little bump in the road," she told the *Detroit Free Press*. "There is still a long way to go."

The following day, the U.S. team faced China. Michele Smith struck out 19 batters and allowed only two hits, but the U.S. hitting slump continued. Once again, the game was an extra-innings disaster that finally ended when a U.S. fielding mistake gave the other team the opportunity to score—and once again, the U.S. team was stunned at the way its chance at Olympic glory was slipping from its grasp. "You've got to score runs to win a ball game," Coach Ralph Raymond told the *L.A. Times*. "We've had some terrific pitching over the last couple of days, but without runs, it means absolutely nothing." The game lasted so long that sprinklers that had been timed to water the grass after the game turned on during the bottom of the thirteenth inning.

The losses put heavy pressure on the U.S. to win its next game, against Australia. The rivalry begun during the 1996 Olympics was still going strong. As in 1996, the U.S.–Australia game was a battle between two great pitchers— Lisa Fernandez and Tanya Harding. Lisa pitched a spectacular game. She struck out 25 batters, a new Olympic record. Like the 1996 U.S.-Australia game, score was 0-0 after seven innings. The U.S. scored in the top of the thir-

Safe! Dot slides into third base as New Zealand's Jackie Smith makes the late tag.

teenth, and victory was almost assured, when, with two outs against her team, Australia's Peta Edebone smacked a two run homcr into the left-field bleachers. Her home run won the game for Australia, 3-1—exactly the way Joanne Brown's had four years earlier.

Nobody could believe it. "If you looked at every face, you would have seen shocking, stunned, searching disbelief," Dot told the *Detroit Free Press.* "A lot of overt tears. Tears of frustration, disbelief, anger, helplessness. Just total solitude . . . "

The U.S., which had been the favorite to win the gold medal, was now in serious danger of going home without any medal at all. After the game, the players focused their energy on driving the bad luck away. In full uniform, they marched into the showers and turned them on full blast to wash the "curse" away. They flushed the toilets to flush the bad luck away. They also passed a softball around. The person holding the softball had to say something positive about herself.

"Everybody talked about what we've been doing good," Dot told the *L.A. Times*. Sometimes when things go badly, we focus on the bad instead of the good."

The team needed to win its next 2 games to qualify for the medal round. " . . . Whatever it takes, we have to believe we will make a difference with the talent we have," said Dot. "We didn't come this far to give up."

The following day, the U.S. started its comeback with a 2-0 victory over New Zealand. Lisa Fernandez finally got her first Olympic hit, and Dot contributed to the victory by driving in a run. Their game against Italy also went smoothly (6-0). The United States had earned a place in the semi-final round—the hard way. Between the U.S. and the gold medal stood the three teams who had beaten them in the semi-final round—China, Australia, and Japan.

" . . . I think that the other teams are not looking forward to playing us but we're looking forward to playing them because they did beat us once and so it's appropriate, and we need, to defeat each and every one of them, to prove that we're really No. 1," Dot told the *L.A. Times*.

After the first round, Japan (7-0) was in first place, followed by Australia (5-2), China (5-3), and the United States (5-3). The semi-final game between the United States and China would determine which team went home without a medal, and which with at least the bronze.

Bringing home the gold, Dot shows off her medal and her team spirit at the 2000 Olympics in Sydney Australia.

With so much at stake, the game was a pressure-cooker. It was difficult to get a player on base, let alone score. After 9 1/2 innings, Stacey Nuveman hit a 3-run homer that gave the victory to the U.S. As in the 1996 gold medal game, the Chinese protested that the ball was foul (it had passed just inside of the left foul pole before landing in foul territory). However, the umpires refused to change the call, and the U.S. advanced to the bronze medal game.

In their next game, the U.S. faced Australia. The winners would advance to the gold-medal game against Japan; the other team would be awarded the bronze medal. Lisa Fernandez pitched for the U.S., and this time, there would be no stunning, extra-inning home runs to yank the win from her fingers. This time, the U.S. wouldn't strand runners on base when it needed them to score. In the fifth inning, with two outs, Dot hit a grounder to center field that drove in a run for the U.S. The U.S. won the game, 1-0.

"Lisa did a great job keeping the ball low, so they were hitting it into the ground," Dot told the *L.A. Times*. "Australia should keep their heads high. We've beaten a great competitor."

The win put the U.S. in the gold medal game against the Japanese, who were undefeated in the tournament. Lisa pitched her second game in a row. At end of seven innings, the score was 1-1. In the bottom of the eighth inning, Stacey Nuveman got on base with a walk. Next up was Dot. She banged out a hit along the right-field line . . . that turned foul. Dot didn't save the day this time, but she did get on base with a walk. Laura Berg stepped to the plate. A long fly ball to center field disappeared into center

Wrapped in the stars and stripes, Team USA defeats Japan to take Olympic gold at the 2000 games.

fielder Shiori Koseki's mitt . . . then popped out of it as Shiori stumbled backwards. Jennifer McFalls sprinted from second, to third, to home to score the game–winning run for the U.S.!

"1996 was the first time softball was ever in the Olympics, and we were very fortunate to have the Olympics in the U.S. But this was one of the greatest challenges for any athlete, and to come to the country of your no. 1 challenger and play them in their backyard is tough," Dot told the *L.A. Times.* "The two were so different from each other, but we appreciate every second of each one."

With her second Olympics behind her, many possibilities lie ahead for Dot. She could be a part of the 2004 Olympic softball team—as a coach.

"The biggest dream is her aspiration to open the Dot Richardson Medical Center," her agent, Tom McCarthy, told the *Orlando Sentinel.* She is now doing a fellowship at Kerlan-Jobe Orthopaedic Sports Medicine Clinic.

"Teaching the game remains the most important thing," Dot said to the *Orlando Sentinel.* "Softball has always been good to me. It allowed the doors of opportunities to open, and I seized those opportunities. If it is time to say goodbye, that I have done all I can, then I will step out gracefully."

Has Dot gone as far as she can go in softball? She once said that the farthest women can go in athletics "is to get a scholarship, and with it an education, and then be a contributor to society for the rest of our lives." Anyone who gives of herself as Dot has can be proud of what she has accomplished.

As her coach Ralph Raymond once told the *Charlotte Observer*, "She has proved to be one of the shining lights in the game of softball."

STATISTICS

	BA	AB	H	R	RBI	HR	OB%	FLD %
1981 UCLA Bruins	.379	177	67	40	13	2	n/a	n/a
1982 UCLA Bruins	.329	137	45	17		0	n/a	n/a
1983 UCLA Bruins	.333	156	52	82		0	n/a	n/a
1996 Olympics	.273	33	9	7	7	3.	306.	962
1999 Pan American Games	.342	38	13	11	6	0.	381	1.000
2000 Olympics	.179	28	5	0	3	1	.303	.909

Olympics and Pan American Games statistics provided by the Amateur Softball Association. Bruins statistics provided by the University of California at Los Angeles (www.ucla.edu).

CHRONOLOGY

1961	Dorothy Gay Richardson is born on September 22 to Kenneth and Joyce Richardson in Orlando, FL
1972	Joins her first softball team, the Union Park Jets, an ASA Class A team
1975	Joins the Orlando Rebels. She is the youngest player ever to play in the ASA Women's Major League Division.
1979	Wins a gold medal at Pan American Games in San Juan, Puerto Rico, the first time that softball is played in the Pan American Games; wins her first Erv Lind award for best defensive player in the national championships; is named an ASA All-American for the first time; attends Western Illinois University
1980	Transfers from Western Illinois University to UCLA
1981	The Orlando Rebels win the ASA national championships; wins her second Erv Lind award
1982	The UCLA Bruins win the NCAA championship; the Orlando Rebels represent the U.S. at the ISF Women's World Championship in Taipei, Taiwan and take fourth place
1983	Wins a gold medal at the Pan American Games in St. John's, Newfoundland, Canada
1984	Receives a bachelor's degree in the study of movement from UCLA; begins playing for the Raybestos Brakettes; wins her third Erv Lind award; is named an ASA All-American
1985	The Brakettes win the ASA national championships
1987	Dot wins a gold medal at the Pan American Games in Indianapolis, Indiana
1988	Receives a masters degree in Exercise Physiology/Health; The Brakettes win the ASA national championships; Dot is named an ASA All-American
1990	The Brakettes win the first of three consecutive ASA national championships
1993	Receives a doctorate in medicine from the University of Louisville
1995	Wins a gold medal at the Pan American Games in Parana, Argentina
1996	Wins a gold medal at the Olympic Games in Atlanta, Georgia; joins the California Commotion; the California Commotion wins the first of four consecutive ASA national championships; Dot is inducted into the UCLA Hall of Fame
1997	Dot completes her orthopedic surgery residency at Los Angeles County/University of Southern California Medical Center;
1999	Wins a gold medal at the Pan American Games Winnipeg, Manitoba, Canada; retires from the California Commotions
2000	Wins a gold medal at the Olympic Games in Sydney, Australia

INDEX

FURTHER READING

Babb, Ron. *Etched in Gold: The Story of America's First-Ever Olympic Gold Medal Winning Softball Team.* Indianapolis, IN: Masters Press, 1997.

Brill, Marlene Targ. *Winning Women in Baseball & Softball.* Hauppauge, NY: Barron's Educational Series, Inc, 2000.

Littlewood, Mary L. *Women's Fastpitch Softball—The Path to the Gold.* Columbia, MO: National Fastpitch Coaches Association, 1998.

Paré, Michael A., ed. "Dot Richardson." *Sports Stars.* Series 3. Detroit: UXL, 1997.

Richardson, Dot. (with Don Yeager). *Living the Dream.* New York: Kensington Books, 1997.

ABOUT THE AUTHOR

HEATHER FORKOS holds a B.A. in English from Bryn Mawr College in Bryn Mawr, PA. She is the author of *Tupac Shakur* in the Chelsea House series "They Died Too Young." She lives in Hanover Park, Illinois.

HANNAH STORM, NBC Sports play-by-play announcer, reporter, and studio host, made her debut in 1992 at Wimbledon during the All England Tennis Championships. Shortly thereafter, she was paired with Jim Lampley to cohost the *Olympic Show* for the 1992 Olympic Games in Barcelona. Later that year, Storm was named cohost of *Notre Dame Saturday*, NBC's college football pregame show. Adding to her repertoire, Storm became a reporter for the 1994 Major League All-Star Game and the pregame host for the 1995, 1997, and 1999 World Series. Storm's success as host of *NBA Showtime* during the 1997–98 season won her the role as studio host for the inaugural season of the Women's National Basketball Association in 1998.

In 1996, Storm was selected as NBC's host for the Summer Olympics in Atlanta, and she has been named as host for both the 2000 Summer Olympics in Sydney and the 2002 Winter Olympics in Salt Lake City. Storm received a Gracie Allen Award for Outstanding Personal Achievement, which was presented by the American Women in Radio and Television Foundation (AWRTF), for her coverage of the 1999 NBA Finals and 1999 World Series. She has been married to NBC Sports broadcaster Dan Hicks since 1994. They have two daughters.

PHOTO CREDITS:

PAGE:
2: Associated Press, AP
8: Associated Press, AP
11: Associated Press, AP
15: Associated Press, AP
16: Jamie Squire/ ALLSPORT
19: Stephen Dunn/ ALLSPORT
24: Associated Press, AP
26: Associated Press, AP

29: Donald Miralle / ALLSPORT
32: Associated Press, AP
34: Associated Press, AP
36: Jamie Squire/ ALLSPORT
39: Andy Lyons/ ALLSPORT
42: Associated Press, AP
46: Andy Lyons/ ALLSPORT

50: Elsa Hasch/ ALLSPORT
53: Associated Press, AP
55: Ezra Shaw/ALLSPORT
57: AFP/Corbis

Front cover photo: Donald Miralle/ALLSPORT
Back cover photo: Nick Wilson/ALLSPORT